AFFILIATE MARKETING

Guide to Making Passive Income from Selling Other People's Products on Social Media

By reading this document, the reader agrees that under no circumstances is the author responsible for any losses, direct or indirect, which are incurred as a result of the use of information contained within this document, including, but not limited to, — errors, omissions, or inaccuracies.

Table of Contents

Chapter 1: Covering the Basics of Affiliate Marketing

Affiliate marketing - you have most likely heard it mentioned in conversations about how to make passive income and wondered what it is exactly, or perhaps you are hearing about it for the first time right now. Either way, affiliate marketing remains one of the most lucrative ventures that you can involve yourself in. It is profitable, it does not demand a whole lot of active involvement, and it can be done by just about anyone who has the right platform. In this first chapter, the basics of affiliate marketing are covered. You will begin to understand what affiliate marketing is, which parties are involved in it, and how to go about getting paid using it. The subsequent chapters explore other important concerns regarding affiliate marketing, such as how to choose the right program, which niches you should be looking into, and how to avoid common mistakes that can lead to failure.

What Is Affiliate Marketing?

What does it mean to be affiliated with something? Merriam-Webster dictionary defines it as being "closely associated with another, typically in a dependent or subordinate position". Affiliate marketing draws from this definition. It is a close association between one big brand (the people whose products you will be selling) and a smaller brand (you). A more detailed definition of affiliate marketing is as follows:

Affiliate marketing is an arrangement whereby a retailer pays a third party commissions for all sales that are brought in by the third party. For every unit of sales generated from the leads that the third party refers to the retailer, there is a proportionate cut or commission that goes into the pocket of the third party.

While affiliate marketing has grown immensely in popularity over the last couple of years, the truth of the matter is that it has been in existence much longer than that. The originator of affiliate marketing as we know it today is a gentleman named William J. Tobin. Tobin is the founder of PC Flowers & Gifts, which is the first-ever platform to run an affiliate marketing program. Under this program, Tobin partnered with Prodigy Network and paid the network a commission for every sale that was made thanks to their input. This type of internet marketing became so profitable that Tobin decided to patent the idea of affiliate marketing. While he applied for a patent in 1996, it was not granted until 2003. Still, this did not stop Tobin from making it to the history books as the very first internet marketer of all time.

After the success of PC Flowers & Gifts affiliate marketing program, other companies started to take a keen interest in this marketing venture. The most famous on the list was Amazon. Amazon became the very first company to offer an affiliate marketing program that was targeted at the general public in 1996. Amazon referred to their affiliate program as Amazon Associates. To date, Amazon's affiliate marketing program remains one of the most popular across the world. Other companies have gone ahead to benchmark and borrow Amazon's model for affiliate marketing for their own use.

Following the emergence and success of affiliate marketing programs, the world needed affiliate networks. An affiliate network is a middleman between affiliate programs and the third parties or publishers. An affiliate network is composed of companies with products that are complementary to each other. As such, these companies are able to refer their customers to each other without losing out on sales. For instance, a company that offers roofing services may refer its customers to a real estate agent and vice versa.

The very first affiliate networks to be formed were the Commission Junction and Clickbank. They opened their doors in 1998 and command a significant share of the market to date. Commission Junction was founded by students from the University of California Santa Barbara while Clickbank was the brainchild of Tim and Eileen Barber.

Since its inception in 1996, affiliate marketing has grown into a $12 billion industry as of the year 2017. It is a lucrative industry that is projected to keep growing for as long as e-commerce continues to be in existence. If you have yet to sign up for affiliate marketing and you own or are capable of owning a digital platform, you are cheating yourself out of a lot of money.

Key Players of Affiliate Marketing

From the brief history of affiliate marketing covered above, it is easy to see that the affiliate marketing machine has several cogs and wheels. In order for this type of marketing to work, there are several key players that must be present. These include the merchant, the affiliate, and the consumer. The network is sometimes included in the list of main players, but in this book, we shall consider the network as having a supporting role.

The Merchant

The merchant plays a crucial role in the affiliate marketing game. The merchant creates the product or service that needs to be pushed through the affiliate program, so without a merchant, those are nonexistent. They call the shots and decide who they get to partner with and how much money their affiliates will earn as commission. The merchant is responsible for providing their affiliates with the links to be placed on the affiliate's websites. They also create ads in the form of content, videos, banners, and even flash ads. The affiliate links provided by the merchant often contain a unique identifier that allows the merchant to determine which sales were referred by which affiliate.

The Affiliate

The affiliate is the party that brings the customers to the merchant. The affiliate's main job is to promote a product or service that the merchant is selling. There are numerous ways of doing this, but all of them are based on the premise of reviewing and recommending an item or service. As an affiliate, you get to determine how much money you make depending on the effort you put into promoting your merchant's products. Chapters 3 and 5 will review some of the steps you can take to convert your audience into buyers.

The Consumer

Another critical cog in the wheel of affiliate marketing is the consumer, without whom there would be no one to sell to. The consumer is the reason why the product or service was created by the merchant in the first place. They have a need that the manufacturer or merchant seeks to fulfill, and they have the money to spend. They probably have loyalties to other companies, so the affiliate must convince the consumer that they need to be spending their money on a particular product and not any other.

Getting Paid from Affiliate Marketing

As mentioned before, the merchant determines how their affiliates will be earning commissions. There are various models that have been adopted to ensure that affiliates get paid from affiliate marketing. Usually, the decision on which model works best is based on what is most beneficial to the merchant.

Pay-Per-Sale

Also referred to as cost-per-sale, this model involves paying the affiliate a commission for every purchase made by a customer that they have referred to the merchant. Some merchants will offer a percentage of the sale as commission while others give a fixed rate for every sale made. A lot of affiliates prefer this model as it allows them to make a good sum of money, especially if they are affiliated with merchants who offer higher priced products. If you choose the right niche, you can very easily make the big bucks with this compensation method. For instance, a 3 percent commission on a high-end device retailing for $3,000 will earn you a cool and easy $90. If you make 20 such sales in a day, you will go to bed with $1,800 of passive income, and that is only for one product.

Pay-Per-Click

This is an easier model, at least on the part of the affiliate marketer. For this one, it does not matter what the customer does once they get to the merchant's link. They may choose to purchase a product or service or not, but either way, you will still get paid for sending them to the merchant's site. A downside of this payment method is that you will only earn a few cents for every click. You will need to have a large amount of traffic if you are hoping to make a reasonable amount of money from affiliate marketing.

Pay-Per-Lead

In the world of internet marketing, a lead is a prospective customer. An affiliate marketing program that is pay-per-lead considers the number of prospective customers that an affiliate brings in to determine what commission must be paid to the affiliate. For a web visitor to qualify as a lead, there must be a supply of contact information that the merchant can use to contact this prospective customer in the future. In other words, if you are an affiliate marketer who is on a pay-per-lead program, you will only get paid if someone signs up on your merchant's website.

Pay-Per-Impression

This type of compensation model is based on how many people are able to see the ads that your merchants display on your website. For this type of model to work well for you, it is important that you have a significant audience and web traffic; otherwise, you might struggle to make a buck.

Which Compensation Method Should You Choose?

At this point, you are most certainly wondering which payment model would work best for you. In an ideal world, you would opt for the model that gives you the most amount of revenue. After all, you are interested in earning enough passive income to make a difference in your life. However, this is often easier said than done. The models that will earn you more money require a whole lot of investment before you can get there. For instance, pay-per-impression requires you to have amassed a great following of people who keep coming back for your content. This is not success that can be achieved overnight.

Pay-per-click is an easier option, because you do not need to convince anyone to buy anything. You just need to lure them into visiting your merchant's website. That being said, you will also need to have sufficient traffic for pay-per-click to work. If you only have 1,000 visitors to your website every month, you will not make a whole lot of money, even if they all click on your merchant's link and visit their site. Assuming you are getting only $0.30 for every click, a month's total earnings would be $300. This is not exactly a bad figure for a beginner, but considering that some people are making millions from affiliate marketing, you should always strive for more. In other words, $300 in earning a month is a good start, but this should not be where you stop.

As such, pay-per-click and pay-per-impression will only work well if you focus on building a great audience. On the other hand, pay-per-lead and pay-per-sale will earn you a lot of money, but you must be prepared to put in the work since a lot of online marketing is required. Pay-per-sale and pay-per-lead are compensation methods that require you to be an astute salesperson. You must be prepared to convince your audience that they need to buy a particular product. Also, you must ensure you create high-quality content that resonates with your audience and cements your credibility. You cannot afford to endorse products that you are not certain about. You will need to be prepared to put your money (and time) where your mouth is.

With that being said, it is important to acknowledge that you need not settle for just one type of compensation method. You may want to choose a combination so that you can cover all your bases. Many successful affiliate marketers are known to combine the models that work best for them. The decision is usually based on the marketer's short- and long-term strategies. If you are not certain about using several models, stick to the one that you are most confident about using.

Are You Ready for Affiliate Marketing? The Ultimate Checklist

How do you get into affiliate marketing? Well, first, you must determine whether you are ready for it. Getting ready for affiliate marketing is a question of checking off all requirements that an affiliate marketer needs to have met before getting into an affiliate program.

- Well-Considered Niche

  What do you love talking about? What do you consider yourself good at? What can you speak about naturally and effortlessly without stumbling over your words? What is the one thing that you feel most passionate about and that you would be comfortable giving a speech about, even if you were awoken in the middle of the night to do so? Answering those questions is how you determine your niche. Choosing the right niche is a critical step in succeeding at affiliate marketing. This first choice will cascade into every decision that you make thereafter. It will inform the partners you choose, the programs you sign up for, and the products that you push to your audience. It will even define the audience that you will be catering to.

Do not make the mistake of getting into a niche simply because everyone else is. Chapter 4 of this book will take a look at some of the most profitable niches in affiliate marketing. Use this chapter as a guide when determining a sub-niche that you can carve out for yourself rather than simply as an argument for certain niches. At the end of the day, only you know what makes you happiest and what you are really interested in. Even if you do not find your niche listed therein, you can still go ahead and invest in it. Maybe the niche that you are interested in is waiting for an independent-minded adventurer like yourself to give it the attention that it requires.

- The Right Channel

For the longest time, websites were the primary channel used in affiliate marketing; however, this is no longer the case. With the rise of numerous social media sites, affiliate marketers have realized the benefits of diversifying their channels with the objective of reaching a larger audience. The channel you ultimately choose will be determined by how you want to approach your affiliate marketing and the audience that you intend to target. For instance, a photographer seeking to partner with a merchant that sells photography gear may choose Instagram as their main channel. If you are into do-it-yourself crafts and love to make videos to document all the crafty things that you are working on, YouTube is a good platform to use. If you get into Etsy's affiliate program, you can include affiliate links in your YouTube video description so that your audience can purchase handmade items from an online store and you can earn commissions.

- The Right Strategy

For any marketing campaign to succeed, there must be an underlying strategy that works to inform the marketing team of what needs to be done, what the long-term objectives are, what milestones to look out for, and so on. Affiliate marketing is not a get-rich-quick scheme that will bring you riches overnight. While it is a technique to earn passive income, you will not be expected to sit passively and wait for the bank to send you an alert. The only passive thing about affiliate marketing is the period after you have put in the work. Think about your favorite blog or website; what do you love most about it? Is it the way the site is designed? Is it the content? Whenever you visit that site, you most likely earn the site some passive income. However, there is a lot of work that went into making sure that the site makes it on your list of favorite websites. In the same way, you must put in the work when coming up with a strategy.

A strategy will involve defining your target audience and target partners, your short term and long term objectives, your marketing methods, your target earnings, an understanding of your competition, keeping up with changing trends, and determining the compensation methods that work best with your objectives and targets.

- The Right Affiliate Program

As you may have noticed so far, affiliate programs are not all alike. There are some that will pay you good money, and there are others that will earn you peanuts. Aside from compensation, affiliate programs also differ in their form of brand reputation. You probably do not want to align yourself with brands that have less than impeccable reputations. Do yourself a favor and find out what customers have to say about a particular brand before you start promoting their products.

- The Right Attitude

Many affiliate marketers often fail as soon as they start. In some cases, this happens because the marketers fail to grasp the concept of affiliate marketing and thus deploy the wrong strategies, resulting in failure. In many other cases, the failure is a result of the wrong attitude toward affiliate marketing. Affiliate marketing is not the gateway to endless wealth. If it were, the Forbes list of the richest individuals would be dominated by affiliate marketers. If you get into affiliate marketing hoping to make $10,000 in the first month, you will be one very disappointed marketer in a month's time. The right attitude in the case of affiliate marketing includes understanding that it will require some time to gain traction before you will start seeing any significant change in your passive income. Give yourself room to learn and grow. If one strategy is not working, consider switching to another. If an affiliate program fails, dip your feet in another; there is no law against experimenting. It is only by trying out different methods that you will figure out what works the best for you and your brand.

Chapter 2: Choosing the Right Affiliate Program

Even before you get into affiliate marketing, you will most likely have a list of niches and programs that you might be interested in. For instance, if you have always been enthusiastic about make-up, you will most likely be hoping to qualify for an affiliate program in the beauty industry. The same goes for anybody who enjoys being outdoors and exploring all the biking trails that nature has to offer. This kind of person will most likely look to align themselves with programs that have a heavy focus on outdoors gear. Though is passion and knowledge all there is to consider when it comes to choosing an affiliate program? Well, these are key considerations, but not the sole factors to think about. If you are looking to land a program that makes you smile all the way to the bank, you'll need to be a lot more strategic.

Tips for Choosing an Affiliate Program That's the Right Fit

With so many affiliate marketing programs claiming to be the best in the industry, getting overwhelmed is to be expected. What's more, there are thousands of reviews on the same ones, which makes the decision-making process even more complicated. If you are new in the affiliate marketing space, you will need to be careful about what program you choose. Deciding upon one that is not the right fit for you and failing at it may discourage you from ever venturing into affiliate marketing again.

If you do not consider any other factors when choosing an affiliate program, make sure that you at least check off each of those listed below:

Choose a program that fits in your niche

Here is the thing - you do not wake up and become an affiliate marketer. You must first establish yourself as a brand that companies want to work with. Sure, a lot of companies will not care much about where you post your link. After all, you get paid whenever your link is used. If your link is not used, it does the companies no harm. However, you want to make sure that your affiliate link does not remain neglected on your website with no visits. The best way to make sure to avoid this is by building a following that trusts you. You will only build a following that believes in your credibility by establishing yourself as an authority figure in a particular niche. Once you have done so and managed to bring substantial traffic to your site, you should sign up for an affiliate program that fits in nicely with your established niche. For example, if you are running a blog that creates content on parenting and motherhood, affiliate yourself with companies that sell baby products, DIY crafts, gadgets that make parenting a little easier, supermarket chains, and so on. However lucrative an affiliate program may be, refrain from choosing it if it does not sit well with your niche. Your audience will see that you are only trying to make cash off of them, and it will not end up well. Such a decision will only dent your credibility and cost you more money in the end.

Promote products that you can use

Do not promote products that you would not use yourself, however tempting they might be. Sure, you may not be able to buy everything before promoting it, but there are some sure signs that a product is not what the manufacturer is trying to make it be. If a product does not make sense to you, you will have a harder time selling it to your audience. Even if you manage to sell it, there is a high chance that there will be returns and complaints, and these can be very damaging to your online reputation. Invest in some due diligence before signing up for an affiliate program. Due diligence does not need to be expensive. You don't have to hire a private investigator for this one; a simple online search and a visit to popular review sites will often give you all the information you need regarding the customers' thoughts on a particular product.

Choose a program that adequately supports affiliates

Just like major chains will offer support to their franchises, you need to choose an affiliate program where you get all the support that you require to conduct a successful promotional campaign. Amazon, for instance, offers simple tools that allow its affiliates to monetize their products regardless of their technical expertise. Walmart, on the other hand, provides a dedicated team whose objective is to help you grow your sales and thus maximize your earnings. While most affiliate programs offer support to their affiliates, there are others that only do the bare minimum (or not even that much) and leave the marketers to their own devices. If you are unable to reach customer service when you need to, this is red flag that you should not ignore.

Another red flag when choosing an affiliate program is any site that has leaks. A leak is anything that cheats you out of your well-deserved remuneration. For instance, let's say that you are signed up for a pay-per-sale affiliate program with a particular merchant.

You create great content and convince some buyers to purchase a product through your affiliate link. Upon arriving at the merchant site through your affiliate link, the prospective buyer realizes that the merchant website has a telephone number that they can call. They call the number, make their order, and buy the product. This is a leak. Even though you led the customer to purchase, you do not get anything from it.

A leak may also occur where you send a buyer to a merchant's site, only for the buyer to find another affiliate link because the merchant is involved in an affiliate program of its own. For instance, let's assume that you are the affiliate of a merchant who sells holiday homes. This merchant is also the affiliate of a tour and travel company. One day, a web visitor is browsing through your site and finds the affiliate link to your holiday homes merchant. While on the holiday homes site, they also realize they can book a holiday through the tour and travel affiliate link. The merchant ends up getting a cut from this while you get nothing. This is another instance where there is a leak that costs you money, and yet you put in the effort in converting a visitor to a buyer.

Many leaks are often the result of ignorance on the merchant's end. With that being said, you should only choose programs that are conscious about putting the interests of all parties involved in the affiliate program at the forefront. This does not mean that merchants should hand over the lion's share to the affiliates. Rather, there should be some mutual consideration that allows both the affiliate and the merchant to draw earnings that are commensurate to the effort they have put in.

Pay attention to the competitors

You are not obligated to stay loyal to any one brand in your affiliate marketing efforts. In fact, a great way of ensuring that you get better commissions is by covering all the bases regarding a particular product. For instance, if you have successfully promoted product A from company X, look at company Y's take on product A. If you can provide your audience with more variety and options, then you stand a better chance at making all of them profitable leads for both yourself and the merchant. In other words, look at the affiliate programs that your merchant's competitors are offering and then sign up for those.

Stay away from affiliate programs that have high return rates

The return rate is defined as the number of orders returned after purchase as a proportion of the total number of sales. For example, if six products are returned for every ten sold, then a merchant is said to have a return rate of 60 percent. High return rates are an indication that a product is not meeting the needs of the customer in that it is defective or lacking in quality. A high return rate might be detrimental to your bottom line, because it means you will get debited for the returns and thus lose your commission. At the same time, if customers have to keep returning products because you oversold their capability, you might be in trouble as far as your reputation as an affiliate marketer. Therefore, it is important to accurately describe what a product can do without making it sound as if it is the solution to all of the world's problems.

Opt for high-end products

Many affiliate marketers who are just starting out are cautious about taking on affiliate programs that require them to promote expensive products. It is natural to wonder whether there is someone out there you can convince to buy a $5,000 handbag. And yet, there are numerous people who would buy the handbag if you sold it to them well enough. If there is a 10 percent commission for this sale, you would be able to comfortably make $500 without breaking a sweat. A great thing about opting for high-end products is that you can really narrow down your target audience and figure out a way of speaking their language. You can implement your affiliate marketing in a way that makes your site seem like an exclusive membership club. Let's say, for instance, that you sign up for an affiliate program to promote boats and yachts. You already know that the people who buy boats have some cash to spare and might also be interested in expensive cigars and designer shoes. They may also love to go on cruises. By profiling your audience, you can keep pushing expensive products and get paid for sales made. The moral of the story is that you should not shy away from high-end or expensive products. You do not have to settle for pennies when you could be running with the big boys.

Ask your audience what they want

Soon after starting your blog or website, you will realize that you are not the boss, but rather, your audience is. They may not come out and tell you that in those very words, but they will show you. If you create content that does not resonate with your audience, you'll get the hint based on the lower traffic that you experience on that day. If you say things that offend your audience, you will notice your subscriber and follower numbers diminishing on a daily basis. Ultimately, your audience will determine how much your brand grows and whether you are successful in your marketing efforts. If your audience holds this much power, then why not ask them directly what they want? Of course, you will not go out and ask them what affiliate marketing program they want you to sign up for. Instead, you will run a poll or survey and ask them what products they would be interested in you reviewing. If a particular product is mentioned several times, look up the manufacturers and find out if they have an affiliate program. Link your affiliate link in the product review, and you will be smiling all the way to the bank.

Compare the payment models and schedules

While you should not be solely motivated by money, you'll want to ensure that you are actually getting paid from your affiliate marketing program and on time. Most affiliate programs have a minimum threshold that you must reach before you can request a payout. The higher the threshold, the longer you might have to wait to get paid. This will ultimately impact your cash flow and might be a problem if you are investing a lot of your own cash into promoting the product. Chapter 1 contains the different compensation models that merchants use and the factors you should consider when choosing an affiliate program as far as payment is concerned.

Go for companies that are well-established

Imagine you are an affiliate marketer already, and you have a nice product that you are promoting. You like the features and functionality of the product and have used it yourself, so you have no problem convincing your followers that they need to buy it. Your audience believes in your credibility and they trust you, so they head onto the merchant's site through your affiliate link. As soon as the prospective customer gets to the merchant's website, they realize that everything is a mess. They cannot navigate the web pages, many product links are broken, and the load times are too long to bear. The prospective customer promptly leaves the site and heads onto another site that is designed better. If you are getting paid per click or per impression, this scenario might not bother you. However, if you are getting paid per sale or per lead, you will truly be bothered. You will begin to wonder why your marketing efforts are not bearing fruit even though you believe in the product you are promoting and the content you are creating. It might take quite some time before you realize that your merchant is the problem.

Established companies have no problem forking out decent money for a high-end website design. e-commerce websites that have been designed well make for a memorable and smooth shopping experience. This is not so for poorly designed websites. The online consumer does not have the patience to wait while a product page loads when they could be spending their money elsewhere. Before signing up for an affiliate program, take a look at the merchant's website and ask yourself whether the website alone would convince you to buy what they are selling. If the answer is no, then you can be sure your audience will not be buying anything either.

At this point, you are probably wondering how to tell whether a website is designed well or not. To the inexperienced eye, all websites look alike or at least seem to look alike. However, the trained eye knows the things to look for when judging a website. Here is what stands out for an e-commerce website that is well done:

It has a clean and crisp design that is not crowded: Imagine trying to shop on a website that is screaming for your attention because of how crowded it is. How would this experience make you feel? Most likely, you would be both annoyed and overwhelmed. Look out for minimalistic approaches when scouring websites. The navigation should be easy, and it is ideal for products to be well-listed without confusing the shoppers.

It can be easily navigated on a mobile phone: According to data released by Statista, 49.7 percent of all online traffic was from mobile devices, excluding tablets. Furthermore, mobile devices accounted for 34.5 percent of all e-commerce sales in 2017. This just goes to show that you cannot ignore the mobile user. A merchant that is running a website that is not optimized for mobile devices is denying themselves a significant portion of the e-commerce pie. Partnering with such a merchant only means that you are also investing in a waste of time, at least as far as the mobile user is concerned.

It allows for swift and easy checkout: No online shopper wants to spend a great deal of time trying to check out. In the physical world, this would be similar to begging a cashier to take your money while they keep sending you straight to the back of the line. There are certain features that make the difference between an easy checkout and a not-so-easy checkout. Ask yourself these questions to determine whether a merchant's checkout process might hinder your earnings as an affiliate:

- Is the checkout button easy to spot?

- Does the merchant have hidden costs that pop up during checkout?

- Is it easy to edit the contents of the shopping cart?

- Does the checkout page load easily and smoothly or are you redirected to other unnecessary pit stops?

- Is the checkout process secure?

It has good product photography: It is for good reason that a wise person once said that a picture is worth a thousand words. A good product photograph can change a buyer's mind and make them purchase something they had not intended to, and a bad one can also do the same but with the opposite effect. Take a good look at the photographs that the merchant has put up and then decide if they look worthy of the price tag.

It has well-written product descriptions: A good product description can make a consumer spend their money without a second thought. Consider this product description: "Nice dress with pleats."

Now, take a look at this alternative description for the same dress: "Vintage, Audrey Hepburn-inspired dress. Comes in three sizes: small, medium and large. Available in white or black. Can be work casual while paired with a well-fitting denim or leather jacket, or can be worn formally with a blazer."

The second description will most definitely have you wanting to take a second look. If you pair this with a crisp product photo, you will have customers pouring in to buy your timeless dress.

Chapter 3: Winning at Affiliate Marketing

Winning at affiliate marketing is well within your reach if you combine the right affiliate program with your very own calculated steps. One of the best things you will ever do for yourself when starting out in affiliate marketing is deciding what channel to work on. At the onset of affiliate marketing, marketers could only hope to make it big on websites. Today's affiliate marketer has a broader range of options including Facebook, Instagram, YouTube, blogs, websites, and even Snapchat. As of the year 2019, there are over 60 social media sites available for you to use in your affiliate marketing efforts. Of course, the demographics of these sites must be considered before a marketer begins to direct their marketing efforts that way. After choosing a channel, you will need to think about how you will direct traffic. How do you pull the crowd and keep them engaged? Social media and internet users as a whole are fickle. They will show an interest one minute and then run away the next. They are a hard crowd to please, and you must be careful about the strategies you deploy to keep them glued.

Choosing the Right Channel

In this section, we will sample some of the channels that you can choose to work on, complete with reasons they would be ideal for you or why they may not be quite what you are looking for.

Website/ Blog

An affiliate marketer does not need to have a website to make a killing in the business. However, a website or blog remains to be one of the best channels for internet marketing as a whole and affiliate marketing in particular. For starters, having a blog or website allows you to build your own independent brand that you can be proud of. Having your own website is not the same as having a Facebook page or group. On your site, you can call the shots and decide what is allowed and what gets vetoed. You can also create blog or web content that is as long as you wish without facing character restrictions as you would on social media sites such as Twitter.

The freedom offered by your own website also means that you can get creative with the type of content that you create. You can create written content and video content as well. You may even choose to have a podcast or sell your own products on the website. It is easy to see that the main advantage offered by a website is the freedom to do whatever you want on your own terms. The downside of having a website is that you will need to make the initial investment of getting it designed, complete with the recurring expense of hosting it and keeping it running. It is important to note that you do not need to spend a lot of money to have a website. There are various platforms that offer software that allows you to design and host your own website without breaking the bank. You do not need to be a website designer to do this; you just need to have an idea of what you want, and you'll be good to go.

Examples of free website builders that will come in handy in your affiliate marketing journey include Wordpress, Wix, Weebly, Jimdo, and SimpleSite. A quick internet search will yield more results, and from those, you should be able to choose a website builder that works for you.

Facebook

Facebook has stood the test of time and held its ground as one of the most popular social media sites of all time. Even though there are reports that Facebook's popularity is declining as a result of newer entrants such as Snapchat and Instagram, the fact still remains that Facebook is a force to be reckoned with. To succeed in affiliate marketing on Facebook, you need to create a significant following. The best way to go about this is either by having a wide friend base (currently capped at 5,000) or a large number of followers. You can get followers on your personal page or on a business page.

You may be wondering how you can create a following on Facebook. As is the case with other channels, you will need to create high-quality content that can be shared by your friends and followers. One great thing about Facebook is that content goes viral pretty easily, especially if it is content that is funny, interesting, authentic, heartfelt, or educational. If you are able to create content that ticks all those boxes, then you have a one hundred percent chance of going viral. Keep in mind that Facebook has approximately 2.4 billion active users per month. This is a significant number that could make your affiliate dreams come true.

Facebook also allows you to boost your page by paying for sponsored ads. You can choose to pay for every click made to your page or per the number of impressions. Whatever option you go for, you will find that the cost of sponsoring your page will be quite affordable compared to traditional advertising costs. For instance, the 2019 cost-per-thousand-views for Facebook advertising is approximately $11.

YouTube

The rise of the YouTube influencer is one that cannot be downplayed. As of the year 2017, YouTube had

1,300,000,000 users. Take a moment to absorb this mind-boggling number, and then imagine how much you could stand to make if only you could convince a small portion of that number to buy products that you are promoting. With some YouTubers taking home millions of dollars, there is definitely room for anybody who wants to get themselves a piece of the pie. It is important to note that the YouTubers who make a lot of money are not necessarily affiliate marketers. Some have made the big bucks through partnering with brands for paid adverts and monetizing their channels so that they can earn from the views they get.

Creating a YouTube channel is easy and free. You will need to have a Google account and then sign into YouTube. While you are signed into YouTube, click on the "Create Channel" button located under YouTube "Settings". While creating a channel is simple and straightforward, getting followers will be more difficult. You can win over followers and subscribers by creating original video content that people love. Unlike written content where you can outsource writers and just copy-paste the end product, video content requires more authenticity. Your audience will be able to see your facial expressions and will know if you are clueless about what you are selling.

A great upside of YouTube when it comes to product reviews and affiliate marketing is that you can visually demonstrate to your audience how a product works. It is one thing to write about how a particular brand of moisturizing facial mask works. Even with the best adjectives, you might fall short of capturing the efficiency of the facial mask. However, with a video, there is irrefutable proof of efficiency and your audience will be more likely to make their own purchase.

Instagram

After its launch in 2010, Instagram has amassed over one billion active users. As far as popularity, it comes in third after Facebook and YouTube. The majority of Instagram users are between the ages of 18 and 34. As such, you will want to be extremely careful when targeting your customers. You must figure out what the needs of this age group are, and then sign up for affiliate programs that fulfill those needs. That is not to say that you should neglect other age groups. In fact, people who are enjoying retirement often have quite a bit of money to spare, and they haven't been left out of the Instagram movement either. The population aged 55 and above accounts for 48 million Instagram users according to user demographics released by Instagram in 2018. Clearly, you still have an opportunity to promote your products to the baby boomers of the world through Instagram.

An important thing to note about Instagram is that, when it comes to content, less is more, at least as far as the written word is concerned. Instagram users are not on the social media platform for the purpose of reading long and elaborate articles about things they don't care about. The appeal of Instagram is in the visual content posted on the platform. If you want to make your mark on Instagram, invest in good photography. Take quality pictures that make your followers want to come back for more. Once you have established yourself as a worthwhile Instagrammer, you can begin promoting your products to your followers.

While you can choose to operate solely on one channel or platform, most affiliate marketers will opt to combine different channels for maximum earnings. Having a well-designed website that is easy to navigate and linked to a popular Facebook page (or vice versa) will earn you more money than you would ever make with just a single Facebook page. Today's online shopper is wiser and more discerning in that they want to gauge your presence across various platforms. Many times affiliate marketers have lost out on commissions simply because interested shoppers could not find their website after a quick Google search. Unless you are a social media influencer who mainly relies on your social media platforms, it is important to combine at least one social media platform with a website.

Driving Traffic to Your Channel

You probably already know by now that the simplest and most organic way to create a following of loyal fans who constantly visit your channel is to provide them with content that is well thought out. However, is this all that is required? Posts that are original and high quality are great, but there is often the question of how to get people to actually find out that it exists in the first place. If you post original content to a new blog that nobody knows about, there is not going to be much traffic regardless of how excellent the quality is.

Guest posts and online publishing

One of the things you'll quickly learn about internet marketing in general is that you cannot exist in isolation, no matter how powerful your brand is. When you are starting out as a blogger or website owner, you'll want to leverage on the visibility offered by other more established sites. You will do this by guest posting on these sites and linking back to your own site. What's more, there are sites that pay you for every article that you guest post, which is a win-win situation for you. Online publishing platforms such as Medium and HubPages are great places for you to share your own original content and draw people to your site.

Guest posting is a team sport in that you will want to make sure that other people are also posting their content on your website. If you can find some industry authority figures, you'll be well ahead of the competition.

Email marketing

Before you dismiss email marketing as old school and ineffective, it is important to note that having the right email marketing campaign has been shown to significantly increase traffic to a site. There are various reasons why many people are not keen on email marketing. For a start, there is the fear of ending up in the spam folder of a mailbox somewhere. Secondly, it can be overwhelming trying to come up with the right email marketing campaign. How long should the email be? What should you include in the body of the email? How do you come up with a catchy email subject? These are questions that can overwhelm a new marketer. A third reason why many marketers shy away from email marketing is a lack of email addresses. If you are not asking your site visitors to provide you with their email address, then you have no way of obtaining this important contact information.

The simplest way of making sure that you get your site visitors' email addresses is by asking for them. However, we all know that most people will not just hand them over unless there is something in it for them. You'll want to ensure that there is an incentive that compels your web visitors to give you their contact information. For instance, if you ask your visitors for their email addresses in order for them to receive a free ebook, there is a better chance that they will actually comply with your request. Aside from offering an incentive, it is important to make sure that the process of entering the email address is simple and straightforward. There are many sites that make customers jump through hoops to supply their email addresses. This often causes the visitors to give up on providing them with this information. Do not fall into this trap. In everything you do while on the internet as a marketer, take the perspective of the customer. The online world, and especially e-commerce, is based on convenience - convenience in accessing information, convenience in shopping, and convenience in organizing through software and online tools. It is about all-around convenience. If something doesn't scream convenience, toss it aside and seek an alternative. Nobody has the time to sign up with a site that makes them go through ten security checks to determine that they are not a robot.

Advertising

People who have well-known and well-established sites do not need to do a whole lot of advertising. Still, most of these sites are never complacent. They make efforts to pay for advertising so that they can reach the population they have yet to penetrate. As a relatively lesser known site that is trying to make inroads, you will need to set aside a budget for advertising. If your site is relatively new or if you have just started out in affiliate marketing on a social media site, you'll want to be careful about the money you put into advertising. You should try to avoid doing too much too soon.

Paid advertising can present quite a significant turnaround for a site that is struggling to get traffic. There are different types of paid advertising, including Facebook ads, Google search ads, and even video ads. Later on, when you have started to make big bucks from affiliate marketing, you can look into investing in more expensive options, such as keyword optimization through Google AdWords.

Remain consistent with your content

Ask anyone who has successfully established an online presence and they will tell you this: the online crowd loves consistency. What does this mean? It means that if you start posting new content on Tuesdays, you must ensure that you have something new every Tuesday. In short, you must train your audience to anticipate new content by establishing a schedule for them. A schedule helps to make sure that you do not have to seek out your visitors every time. Instead, your visitors will be the ones refreshing your page to see whether there is something new that needs to be read or watched. After establishing a consistent posting schedule, you can further hook your visitors by asking them to give you their email addresses. This way, you can notify them every time you have new content so they never miss a thing. Of course, this will be a clever way of getting email addresses (which you can use for email marketing as discussed above) without seeming too obvious about your intentions.

Optimize your website

In internet marketing, there is a phenomenon known as search engine optimization. Abbreviated as SEO, search engine optimization in the simplest terms refers to the techniques that ensure your site doesn't get lost in the vastness of the internet. When a visitor types words or phrases into a search engine, they usually only look at the sites listed on the first page of the search engine results. If your website or blog always comes up on the second, third, or fourth page, then you will have a hard time winning at affiliate marketing. Title tags, meta descriptions, and keyword phrases are examples of simple SEO techniques that you can implement on your website to give it a visibility boost. If you are severely lacking in SEO know-how, you might want to hire an SEO expert to give you some tips and guidance on what is lacking on your website and how you can counter this. Oftentimes, it is best to bring in the search engine optimization expert at the website design phase so that their suggestions can be incorporated into the organization of your site. You do not want to overhaul a website that is already up and running as this may interfere with the user experience.

Get Out of your house

Becoming an affiliate marketer is not the excuse you need to stay holed up in your house. If you want to win at affiliate marketing, you will need to get out of your comfort zone and rub shoulders with other players in the industry. At any one time, there is a networking event happening somewhere that might be relevant to you. Do yourself a favor and make a habit of attending at least one networking event every two months. You'll be surprised at the kind of leads you will get from such events. Word of mouth marketing is very effective, and many people will be curious to check out your website after talking to you in person. They'll want to put a website to the face, so to speak.

Ask your audience to share your content

Whenever you post content or affiliate links on your website or blog, make a habit of asking your audience to share the same with their friends and followers. This simple call to action can have quite an impact. Do not just assume that your followers will share your posts or videos with the people they care about.

Remind them to do so; may be surprised at the uptick in traffic that will result from this. Of course, you'll have to be certain that you make sharing easy by linking your content with social media sites such as Facebook and allow the option of sharing via email.

Hire someone to do the heavy lifting

You do not have to get consumed by your affiliate marketing venture. If you have a website that is functional and that has a steady following, you can outsource the running of the website to a third party. It can be particularly stressful to run an affiliate marketing program while also paying attention to your day job. Fortunately, there is no shortage of people to help. Platforms such as Upwork and Freelancer allow you to hire qualified and experienced virtual assistants and social media marketers who can take some of the load off you. Of course, you'll want to make sure that you are stepping in regularly for quality control, but this way, you don't have to worry about the tiny details, such as ensuring that posts are scheduled on time or that questions are replied to when required.

Avoid sounding like a broken record

As an affiliate marketer, it is important to avoid sounding like a pushy salesman who is desperate to make a sale at any cost. The best way to convince your audience to buy a product is by letting them know what the product can do for them and then stepping back to allow them enough room to make the decision to buy or not buy. If you have done your homework well and put together a killer product review that covers all the bases, you will have a very easy time converting your leads. If you have put together fluff for the purpose of presenting something to your audience, then you will lose their attention midway through your pointless content. Some of the best affiliate marketers in the world are those that point out the benefits of a product and the discounts and rewards that you stand to gain when you make a purchase; they then walk on their merry way. They have confidence in their content and know that they need not stand behind you whispering in your ear and begging you to make a purchase. This confidence is further reinforced by the assurance that the product they are promoting is of high quality, which underlines why you should always begin your affiliate marketing journey with a product that you believe in.

Chapter 4: Best Affiliate Marketing Niches for Big Bucks

While money should not be the sole consideration when choosing an affiliate program, the truth of the matter is that it is a crucial factor. Some affiliate programs are a waste of money and energy because they do not give you any significant return on your investment. You will experience more satisfaction if you choose a program that can pay you back for all the effort and money that you invest in setting up your marketing platform and strategies. There are niches that are more likely than others to provide you with the big bucks. Read on to find out which niches these are. Remember that you should not choose a niche simply because it has the possibility of earning you a lot of money. After reading through this list, think about one or two niches that would interest you the most. It is important to make sure that you can speak intelligently about a niche before you dive into it.

1. **Pet business**

   Did you know that cat videos are one of the most popular types of videos on the internet? If you have a hard time believing this, just do a quick search for cat videos on YouTube. Most of the videos that have anything to do with cats have amassed millions of views. People really do love animals; they love to watch them being cute and adorable, and they also enjoy the occasional naughtiness of our four-legged companions. When it comes to spending money, many people have no qualms with splurging on their pets. The American Pet Products Association carried out a survey in 2017 and found that Americans had spent $70 billion dollars on their pets in the same year. The majority of this amount ($29 billion) went to pet food, while $6 billion went to pet services like grooming. As you can see, you don't even need to convince people that they should spend money on their pets; you just need to show them why they need to buy a particular product, and you will earn some money.

2. Beauty

The beauty industry will always be one of the most profitable industries of all time. In 2017, the global beauty industry was valued at over $500 billion. This figure is expected to rise to over $800 billion by the year 2023. Like the pet business, you do not need to convince people to spend their money on beauty products. The media has already done plenty of that by setting unattainable beauty standards. Every day, there is a woman somewhere who wants to get rid of their wrinkles and look younger than they really are, and there is a man convinced that he can win over more ladies by applying an anti-aging serum or cleansing their face with an all-improved charcoal cleanser. You just have to know where to find these consumers and then convince them that the serum you are selling is the best on the market. How do you loop them in? By creating catchy content and highlighting what is in it for them. People like to know that a particular product was created to solve their problems and not to take their money.

3. Health and wellness

Everybody wants to feel and look good. Regardless of where you are in your life, there is always something that you feel could use some improvement. This is a sentiment shared by a lot of people across the world. The health and wellness industry is touted to be the next trillion-dollar industry. Imagine the amount of money you stand to make by investing in such an industry where the meteoric rise is nowhere near its end and where demand is plentiful, so you will not need to be pushy about selling your products. You only need to establish yourself as an authority figure. Consumers love to know that they can trust you. If you are a consumer of the industry yourself, you are one step ahead of the bunch. For example, if you have good things to say about a health supplement that has changed your life, consumers will trust that you have crucial insider knowledge and will likely buy whatever it is that you are promoting.

4. Fashion

Without a doubt, fashion was going to make it on the list. Why do you think Dolce & Gabbana is such a big brand? People love fashion. Many people view it as a way of making a statement while defining their self-identity. Even those people who claim to not bother themselves with fashion have a little part of them that does care about style. After all, there is something in a person that influences them to pick a particular outfit over another. There is always a message that is communicated by fashion. You just need to figure out what this message is and then convince your audience that they can convey their message better by choosing the clothing brand that you are promoting.

5. Gadgets

The modern world is currently obsessed with gadgets. Everywhere you turn, there seems to be a manufacturing company competing to give consumers the newest and most high-end gadget. The good news is that consumers are willing to spend money. There are people who believe that one good gadget is suitable for a lifetime. As such, they will buy a good phone and use it for as long as they can before replacing it. Lucky for you, this is not how the majority of the population thinks. Just take a look at Apple; since the invention of the iPhone, the company has released 18 versions of the iPhone. Despite the fact that most of these phones have the same functionality and work pretty much the same way, folks continue to throw their money at the latest and most currently updated model. However, it is not only phones that people are obsessed with. Smart watches, smart TVs, fitness devices, and high-end cameras are just a few examples of gadgets that can help you win at affiliate marketing. Because of the very technical nature of these devices, you will need to be extremely careful with the content you curate for your audience. You cannot merely put up an article that says a particular gadget is 'nice, and easy to use'. People who spend thousands of their hard-earned dollars on techy gadgets want to be impressed by your knowledge. Make sure you sound smart and authoritative. Before you start promoting a particular tech gadget, be certain you know its pros and cons like the back of your hand.

6. Investment

They say that money is not the key to happiness, but this has never stopped anyone from wanting to have more money. Most people work hard for their earnings and want the assurance that it is working hard for them in return. Unfortunately, a majority of people do not know where to invest their money; that's where you come in. There are many investment options that you can promote as an affiliate marketer. These include trading platforms such as eToro which invest in stocks, commodities, and high-interest savings accounts offered by reputable banks and other banking platforms. If you can establish yourself as an authority figure in the field of investment and even show your audience how you have benefited from investing, you will be one step ahead when it comes to winning a solid following. Investment facilities that work with affiliate marketers often offer flat fee commissions or a commission for every lead that you generate. The commissions are often decent enough to guarantee you a substantial passive income. They are often in the range of $100 to $200 and are offered per unit (e.g. per account opened, per leads generated, and so on).

7. **Credit facilities**

Thanks to the high cost of living, loans have become a favorite for many people. From personal loans to business loans and everything in between, credit facilities continue to be one of the most preferred ways of fixing financial emergencies. Banks and other lending facilities know this and are always competing with each other for customers. As such, lending facilities are on the lookout for affiliate marketers who can promote their products to the masses. Most people do not like being in debt unless they think doing so is going to solve a particular problem that they have. For this reason, many lenders have devised clever ways of enticing people to take out loans. As an affiliate marketer, you have to create content that helps your audience understand why they need to take out a particular loan. You must also target them strategically so that you are speaking to a demographic that is actually interested in loans. College students who are about to graduate, for instance, may be interested in loans that help them refinance their student debt. However, freshmen may not be too keen on this. Young adult professionals may be looking to buy their first house while older folks may want to take out a loan for home improvement and so on. It is all a matter of understanding what your audience's pain points are and then giving them the all-important solution.

8. Outdoor gear

You can make some big bucks promoting products that outdoor enthusiasts are looking to buy. There is a population of people out there who derive great joy from being outdoors and are willing to buy the gear required to make this possible. Whether you are talking about camping gear, hiking equipment, or even fishing gear, there is a great demand for all things outdoors. Again, seeing how this is an area that is rather esoteric, you will need to ensure that you know what you are talking about. If you are promoting fishing gear, for example, at least make an effort to understand the basic differences between baitcasting reels and fly fishing reels so that you don't get caught with your foot in your mouth. You do not need to be enthusiastic about all outdoor activities (though this does help), but you do need to demonstrate a bit of knowledge in these areas.

9. Self-improvement

Most people have something in their life that they struggle with and that they are hoping to improve. This could be their personal relationships, work-life balance, self-esteem, parenting techniques, mental and emotional issues, or even school-related issues. You can name any one thing under the sun and there will be someone struggling with it. This is why the self-improvement industry is so huge. There is no shortage of motivational speakers who are looking to help people change an aspect of their life. There are several self-improvement affiliate programs that you can choose from, including platforms that have self-improvement courses, such as INeedMotivation, publishers of self-improvement books, including Hay House, and even websites of public speakers and inspirational figures, such as Brian Tracy, who is the founder and chief executive of Brian Tracy International.

10. Fitness and weight loss

This niche falls under health and wellness, but it is so distinct in terms of demand and industry value that it requires a section of its own. Under this category, there are numerous ways that you could tailor your approach. For instance, you might want to specialize in being an authority figure for moms who want to lose weight after childbirth or even men in their mid-forties who want to get their groove back. Whatever way you want to approach this, the main concern is to ensure that you do not get too general. There are many reasons why people are interested in fitness and weight loss. You cannot be the panacea to all those reasons. You will not be able to juggle between being the authority figure for competitive bodybuilding, being the authoritative voice for weight loss after surgery, catering to young males in their twenties, and everything else in between. If you do this, you risk losing your focus and confusing your audience. Pick one path and stick to it. Let people associate you with a certain specialty, such as the weight loss guy who helps girls feel better after gastric bypass surgery or the healthy weight gain guy. In picking a niche, you will also be carving a strong suit for yourself from within. Do it wisely.

Chapter 5: Common Pitfalls to Avoid in Affiliate Marketing

If you're looking to succeed in affiliate marketing (which should be your objective right from the start), you must be careful not to make some mistakes. There are a whole lot of misconceptions surrounding affiliate marketing. Hopefully, by this point in the book, you are able to easily tell what is and is not true about affiliate marketing. For instance, affiliate marketing is not a get-rich-quick scheme if you do not want to do the heavy lifting. Success in affiliate marketing requires you to put in consistent work. This is the only way you are going to differentiate yourself and stand out from the crowd. With so many people taking to affiliate marketing as a preferred source of passive income, you will require grit and determination to get ahead.

Let's take a look at some of the most common mistakes people make when it comes to affiliate marketing:

1. **Choosing the wrong product**

    There are several reasons why a person might pick the wrong products to be affiliated with. You may choose a product simply because you think there is a lot of money in it. While earning money is a motivator to get into affiliate marketing, making it the sole consideration sets you up for failure. If you pick a product simply because you have heard that other people have made big bucks from it, you might struggle to find passion when marketing this product. In Chapter 2, we looked at the different factors that you should think about before settling on an affiliate program. Feel free to refer to this chapter for a refresher.

2. Not being proactive

Just because you are affiliated with a major brand does not mean that you can sit back and wait for online traffic to drive itself to your website. A lot of affiliate marketers make this mistake without realizing that they are just one of many. Customers have a lot of options to choose from when it comes to deciding where to take their business. You must be committed to ensuring that you give customers a unique experience that makes you an easy choice for them. Social media marketing and search engine optimization are two examples of techniques that you can use to drive traffic to your website.

3. Doing too much

It can be very exciting to watch the money trickle in from your affiliate marketing programs. When this happens, you might want to get into as many affiliate marketing programs as you can. The desire to maximize profits is a natural part of being an entrepreneur. However, this desire should not turn into greed whereby you sign yourself up for all the affiliate programs that you can get your hands on. If you do this, your website users will find themselves in a position where the ads outnumber the content on your page. This can be very off-putting and will often be counterproductive. Do yourself a favor and stick to a reasonable number of programs. Don't be the guy who is everywhere, doing everything at all times. Nobody trusts this guy.

4. Being lazy or stingy with content

The importance of content in affiliate marketing cannot be overemphasized. Content is what draws traffic to your website, and it is what ensures that your website users keep coming back long after they have figured out what the product you are promoting is all about. Do not be lazy with content. If you are not feeling very creative, hire someone to take care of your content for you. Have a consistent schedule for posting so that your readers and customers know when to anticipate new material. Make sure that all the content that you post is interesting and educative; nobody wants to read fluff or bare facts and statistics that are boring. Find a way of striking the all-important balance between informative and fun, and you'll be well on your way to establishing yourself as an authority figure in your niche.

5. Poorly done website

Nobody wants to visit a website that they'll struggle to navigate. Every time a visitor visits your website, you have a thirty-second window during which time you'll convince them to stay and explore or leave and never come back. Considering the fact that over 50 percent of all e-commerce comes from mobile devices, an important question to ask yourself is whether your site is optimized for mobile phones. There are various ways of ensuring that your website is well optimized to suit the needs of mobile users. One such way is by having a mobile app version of your website. This way, users can easily access your site while on the go. It will also be necessary to ensure that your pages open quickly on mobile devices so users don't spend precious minutes waiting for content to load. A simple way to go about ensuring your site is friendly to mobile users is to enlist the help of web designers. Most of the designers on the market today offer comprehensive design packages that allow you to get topnotch sites that are friendly for both mobile and desktop users.

6. Unwillingness or inability to measure performance

So you have set up a website and signed up for several affiliate programs. You can tell that there are some visitors making it to your site thanks to the comments left behind and the purchases done through your affiliate link. This is hardly enough, though. As an affiliate marketer, your best bet when it comes to determining your performance is doing deliberate tracking and measurement of performance. It is crucial that you determine how well you are doing as an affiliate marketer. Relying on gut instinct and the occasional payment from your affiliate program will not give you a comprehensive picture of what is actually happening.

There are several tools that you can utilize to measure your performance. One such tool is Google Analytics, which allows you to track and monitor your website traffic. It gives you the capability of identifying patterns in your marketing campaign, thus enabling you to make informed decisions. For example, you can tell which content is most popular among your users, where the majority of your traffic comes from, and even how long your users stay on your site before taking their business elsewhere. Successful affiliate marketing requires that you stay on top of the game with the right data and information. You cannot afford to make guesses and hope that you land on the right answers. Do yourself a favor and measure your efforts. Remember that you can only manage what you are measuring.

7. Being reluctant to learn

The online world is highly dynamic. The tips and tools that work today may not necessarily work tomorrow. As an affiliate marketer, educating yourself consistently is the only way to ensure that you are not caught off guard. Even if you are currently the most successful affiliate marketer, there is bound to be a new kid on the block who will topple you and take over your position if you allow yourself to get too comfortable. A good thing about the trends that you need to take note of is that all the information you require is well within your reach. You just need to ensure that you subscribe to the right channels that have updated information, and you'll be good to go. Networking with other players in the market is another way of ensuring that you do not fall behind when it comes to news and information.

8. Sticking to what you know

There is a certain comfort to sticking to what you are used to. If you have always done things a particular way, it can be very disconcerting trying to change things up. Change may be as good as rest but change is also scary and unpredictable. For example, if you have been creating written content, you might want to spruce things up with video content and see what happens. The same applies to sending the same type of email day in and day out. However much your contacts love reading your emails, there will come a time when they will get tired of the same exact kind of formatting. Spice things up by alternating between HTML and plain emails, and see what happens. If the switch does not work, you can always go back to your old style. The important thing is that you will have tried.

9. Ignoring your competition

As an affiliate marketer, there is a lot that you can learn from your competition. Benchmarking with the competition is a great way of identifying what works best and what does not work as well. Your competitors know a thing or two that you may not know. Feel free to snoop a little on what the other side is up to; it is a normal and expected part of the business. Big brands and companies do so all the time and so should you.

10. Going with the flow

Just because your competition is doing something does not mean that you must do it. As an affiliate marketer or blogger, you must also challenge yourself to come up with authentic ways of strengthening your brand and position. Having the right strategies is a crucial part of succeeding in affiliate marketing. These strategies will not always be public information. Many times, you will need to be creative and think outside the box. Some of the best promotion strategies were thought up by someone who realized that there was something missing, and so they decided to be innovative. You can be that person.

Chapter 6: Most Popular Affiliate Programs and Networks of 2019

There are some affiliate programs that tend to be more popular among marketers than others. Often the popularity is largely driven by the amount of earnings that the marketers derive from them. Other factors that may influence the popularity of an affiliate program can include things such as the kind of support offered by the merchant, the brand position, the reputation of the merchant, and the ease of transactions between the affiliate and the merchant. This final chapter takes a look at some of the most popular affiliate programs of 2019. If you are looking to get started with affiliate marketing right away, these ten programs are a good place for you to begin.

#1: Amazon Associates

Amazon's affiliate program is a great choice for a person who is just getting started in affiliate marketing, as there are millions of products that you can choose from. Data released in 2017 showed that Amazon lists over one million products on a daily basis. In total, as of 2017, Amazon had a product catalog of over 600 million products. Needless to say, this number has risen in the period between 2017 and now. With such a wide range of options, you are most definitely going to find something that is relevant to your niche. Another great thing about Amazon's affiliate program is that you do not need to do a whole lot since the bigger part of the sales process is handled on Amazon's end. Your only job will be to make sure that your audience gets to Amazon. After that, Amazon deploys its enticing sales techniques and converts your lead into a customer. At the end of it all, you will receive a commission that is based on their commission structure. The commission rates range from 1 to 10 percent, depending on the category of the product.

#2: eBay Partner Network

eBay's affiliate program allows you to earn a percentage of revenue for every sale that a customer you refer makes. According to their website, this percentage is anywhere between 50 and 70 percent, depending on the category of the product purchased. By signing up for eBay Partner Network, you will have access to simple linking tools that allow you to easily promote products to your followers. You will also get access to a dashboard that allows you to track your leads and earnings per sale. It is important to note that you will only earn money if a customer makes a purchase within 24 hours of accessing eBay through your affiliate link. If this time expires, you might lose out on a commission from the sale.

#3: Shopify

Shopify's affiliate program promises to help you earn up to $2,000 for every customer you refer. What exactly is Shopify, though, and why are they able to pay such mind-boggling sums of money to their affiliates? Launched in 2008 by three gentlemen based in Canada, Shopify is a site that helps you set up an online store through which you can advertise, sell, and ship your products. Shopify allows online sellers to bypass the costly hassle of setting up e-commerce websites. The affiliate program gives you access to online content and support from the Shopify team on top of ensuring that you earn money every time a customer signs up for a Shopify store. With an increasing number of people selling their products online, you stand a good chance of making some decent money through Shopify's affiliate program.

#4: ClickBank

ClickBank is an affiliate program, or more accurately, it is an affiliate network that deals solely with digital content. The range of products available on ClickBank includes ebooks, lessons and tutorials, recipes, games, dating products (such as self-help and self-improvement material), weight loss and fitness products, and just about anything else that can be converted into digital format. (There are physical products, as well, but these do not make up the majority.) An advantage of ClickBank is that it is an affiliate marketplace, or a middleman, that brings together content creators and marketers. By signing up for ClickBank, you will be taking on half of the work (they have done the other half) and commissions of up to 75 percent. ClickBank allows you to quickly find things to promote since it consolidates millions of products in one place. The fact that their website is very easy to navigate is another reason why it is such a good choice for a beginner. If you are looking to get your affiliate marketing feet wet, give ClickBank a go.

#5: ShareASale

ShareASale is yet another affiliate marketing program that helps you easily find merchants whose products you can promote. Instead of searching high and low for merchants that fit your niche and ideals, you can opt to choose the one-stop shop that is ShareASale. Unlike ClickBank which focuses mainly on digital products, ShareASale lists physical products, including clothing and apparel, home improvement products, and services like website design and photography. Signing up to ShareASale affiliate program also gives you access to around 1,000 merchants that are exclusively listed on this particular affiliate program. What this means is that if you are interested in partnering with any of these merchants, you can only access them through ShareASale.

#6: TripAdvisor Affiliate Program

It's likely that you have used TripAdvisor at some point in your life. Launched in 2000, TripAdvisor has become the go-to site for people who want to find out how a particular travel destination, hotel, or restaurant measures up. If you are a travel blogger or are keen on traveling, TripAdvisor's affiliate program may interest you. You are probably wondering why a review site would need an affiliate program when they clearly do not sell a product. While TripAdvisor is indeed a review site, it also has partners in the form of hotels, restaurants, and airlines. When you sign up for their affiliate program, you are essentially signing up to help TripAdvisor sell travel packages to customers in the form of accommodation, travel, and so on. TripAdvisor's affiliate program is run by CJ Affiliate.

#7: CJ Affiliate

CJ Affiliate runs one of the most recognized affiliate networks in the world. Established in 1998, CJ Affiliate currently boasts over 3,000 brands with an impressive catalog of millions of products. Aside from giving you access to some of the top brands in the world, CJ Affiliate also offers tools that will make your affiliate marketing journey much easier. These tools include real-time monitoring dashboards and even automatic link generation, which saves you the time that you would otherwise use to embed links manually. CJ Affiliate is a bit strict in their requirements as they require you to have a site that has useful content. They also do not take kindly to slackers; performance is reviewed after six months, and if you are found to be falling behind, then you might be kicked out of their affiliate program.

#8: Hotels.com Affiliate Program

Hotels.com, as the name might suggest, is a site that contains listings of hotels across the world. It allows you to book your accommodation conveniently and securely, while also giving you access to discounts that every traveler can use. Their affiliate program is relatively simple and straightforward; you sign up and earn every time someone books a room through your link. At 4 percent, the rates offered by Hotels.com may not be as high as those in other programs. However, they are a good start for anyone who wants to practice a little affiliate marketing before getting into the big leagues. In order to earn through this affiliate program, a booking has to be made within seven days of accessing your affiliate link. Therefore, you will want to make sure that your web visitors use their link urgently. A clever way of doing so might be by mentioning that they stand to gain discounts and rewards if they make a booking within a seven-day period. You can determine what reward to give based on what would be cost-effective given the circumstances (that is, the 4 percent commission rate).

#9: WordPress Affiliate Program

Does creating your own site on WordPress and then getting paid for telling other people to create their sites on WordPress sound appealing to you? The fact that WordPress provides you with such an easy way to create a website means that you will not have a very difficult time convincing people to sign up. With so many people asking how to create a website of their own (either for blogging purposes or for e-commerce), you can step in and answer this question and get paid in the process. A clever way of enticing your site visitors into using WordPress is by putting up a video explaining how to go about creating a WordPress site. Yes, WordPress has its own videos doing this, but there is a difference between the one you create and the one that comes from the website builder. With your video, there is the added benefit of first-hand user experience and the comfort of the rapport you have built with your online community. This affiliate program promises to earn you up to 20 percent for every person you refer that becomes a paying customer.

#10: Rakuten Marketing

Rakuten Marketing works with big brands such as Walmart, Sephora, and Best Buy, among others. The company has held the title of the top affiliate marketing network for eight years in a row, and, according to their website, they have fulfilled over 110 million orders worldwide. Rakuten is a good place to start for the go-getter who is not afraid of swimming with the big sharks. A good thing about this affiliate marketing network is that you will be provided with all the tools that you require, and all you need to do is ensure that you put them to good use. Rakuten Marketing offers high-quality products, which means that making sales and getting decent payouts is relatively easy. They also offer ongoing support and training for their affiliates. On the downside, Rakuten Marketing does not approve inexperienced affiliates. You will need to demonstrate your capacity and track record before you will be allowed to join this rather exclusive club.

Of course, this list is not comprehensive of all affiliate programs that exist. If you perform a quick Google search, you would discover that it is only a tiny tip of the iceberg. There happen to be thousands of affiliate marketing programs that you can choose from. If you are feeling overwhelmed by the process of deciding on the right one for you, refer back to Chapter 2 for some tips regarding what to consider when choosing the ideal affiliate program.

Conclusion

Whether you rely on social media or have an up-and-running website, you can earn passive income by choosing to be an affiliate marketer. As an affiliate marketer, you do not have to worry about coming up with innovative products or putting money into a manufacturing process. The hard work of product development and production is taken care of by a third party, allowing you to focus on the more interesting role of convincing consumers that they need to spend their money on a particular product. While this might be difficult at the beginning, it often happens that people learn to trust you, especially if you consistently push products that are high in quality and value-added.

If you have always wanted to get into affiliate marketing, this book is the gentle push that you have been waiting for. As you may have guessed by now, there is nothing complicated about affiliate marketing. You just need to be calculating in the steps you take concerning choosing an affiliate program, deciding upon a channel or platform, and creating content for your audience. When you have taken care of the basics, everything else is bound to fall into place.

So, get started today! If you do not have a website, start with your Facebook page. If you have a robust YouTube channel where you broadcast your interests and everyday life, take advantage of the fact that there are already people paying attention, and sell to them. Let them know why they need a certain product or service in their life. If you make a good case, you can count on making a decent passive income that can help you offset some of your bills or pay for a well-deserved vacation.

References

New Thrive Learning Institute. (2016). *Affiliate Marketing - the Complete Affiliate Marketing Handbook.*: Lulu.Com.

Gray, D. (2000). *The Complete Guide to Associate and Affiliate Programs on the Net*. New York: McGraw-Hill.

Weaver, J. (2013). *Manager's Guide to Online Marketing*. New York: McGraw-Hill.